THE

CONNECTION FACTOR

FOR

WOMEN

UNLOCK THE POWER OF PURPOSEFUL CONNECTIONS

CYNTHIA CHIRINDA

Wholeness
Incorporated
Publishing

The Connection Factor for Women
Unlock the Power of Purposeful Connections
Copyright © 2025 by Cynthia Chirinda
Originally published in 2018 under the title *The Connection Factor: Connections that Unlock the Potential of the Whole Woman*
Revised and rebranded edition © 2025 Cynthia Chirinda
All rights reserved.

Scripture quotations, unless otherwise noted, are taken from the Holy Bible, King James Version (KJV).

Original Cover design by Tapiwa Kahonde.
Revised layout and design by Annie Nyamudzwadzuro
Published by Wholeness Incorporated
Harare, Zimbabwe

For coaching, consulting, author resources, or speaking engagements, visit:
www.cynthiachirinda.com
info@cynthiachirinda.com

ISBN: 978-0-7974-9760-3

CONTENTS

DEDICATION

To every woman who is determined to overcome adversity on her journey to pursuing wholeness.

ACKNOWLEDGEMENTS

I extend my heartfelt gratitude to the many women who have strengthened my resolve in life by allowing themselves to be vulnerable in sharing their journeys.

To my Heavenly Father—God Most High—who enables me to walk in intimate fellowship through a relationship brokered by the Lord Jesus Christ and sustained by the power of the Holy Spirit, I give You all the glory and honour.

INTRODUCTION

Women are often misunderstood—by their actions, words, and even silence. In my own journey as a woman, I have come to realise that it takes a resilient spirit and a healthy self-image to navigate life with courage and authenticity.

Many women live through layers of shock, humiliation, abuse, betrayal, and emotional pain, yet are expected to show up, hold space for others, and nurture life. In the process, they may lose connection with their core identity—defined not just by roles, achievements, or appearance—but by their sacred purpose and potential.

Some of the experiences we endure carry deep shame and unspoken grief, creating internal prisons that block intimacy, growth, and self-expression. Others suffer silently in relationships that drain, diminish, or dominate them. Yet even in those dark places, a flicker of wholeness calls us home.

Healthy relationships are meant to anchor us, inspire growth, and offer spaces of joy, belonging, and restoration. But dysfunctional connections—whether romantic, social, spiritual, or professional—can become places of emotional bondage and soul erosion. It is within this tension that we must pause, reflect, and courageously audit our connections.

Women are the spiritual and social fabric of our communities. When women thrive, families heal, generations transform, and nations rise. But when we as women remain broken, suppressed, or disconnected from ourselves and each other, we risk perpetuating cycles that keep our potential buried.

Oppression of women is systemic, often masked in tradition, law, religion, and the media. It targets our reproductive capacities, distorts our self-worth, and seeks to silence our power. But God, who fearfully and wonderfully crafted us, invites us into a journey of identity, purpose, and healing that transcends external limitations.

This book is an invitation—a mirror to examine your life through the lens of connection. You were not created to exist in isolation, nor in cycles of wounding and worthlessness. You were designed for wholeness.

May you find the courage to reconnect with the divine blueprint of your womanhood, to nurture meaningful bonds, and to rise into every season fully awakened, fully loved, and fully you.

To Your Wholeness,

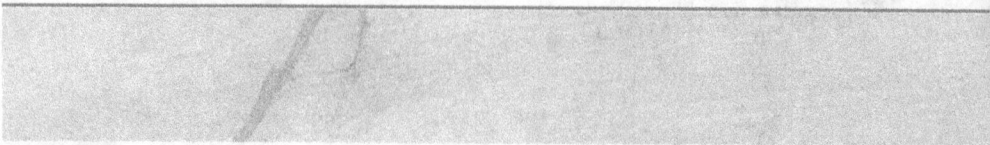

THE
CONNECTION FACTOR
FOR
WOMEN

UNLOCK THE POWER OF PURPOSEFUL CONNECTIONS

CHAPTER
ONE

RETURN TO INNOCENCE

THE JOURNEY OF TAMBUDZAI

The sun's glistening rays filtered through her eyes and cast a shadowy print on the beautiful mulberry tree above her. A gentle breeze scathed away teasingly at her frilly lace top on her shrivelled bent frame. She shuddered a little but did not flinch or move. She continued to gaze deeply in the far distance as if trying to make sense of what was approaching her. The tall grass around her compound began to sway and whistle gently as though to call her back to the present, but she continued to stare blankly with unperturbed focus, as she silently recollected her spent years. In the midst of the noise of the barking dogs chasing after the errant neighbour's kitten, Magumbo, in her ears these were just but muted echoes as she pierced the impending darkness with her sharp eyes.

Tambudzai's story is one of hope, heartbreak, betrayal, and resilience. It is a testimony of the woman who dared to dream of a different life but found herself caught in a maze of sorrow and disconnection. Born and raised in rural Zimbabwe under her grandmother's care, Tambudzai's early years were shaped by hardship and longing. An orphan from birth, she grew up carrying water, fetching firewood, and living in the shadow of her grief. Yet, she harboured dreams of love, purpose, and escape from the daily pain that had marked her childhood.

Her world turned when MuJubheki—once known as Toringepi—returned to their village, a long-lost son who had disappeared after a youthful conflict. Their love story blossomed like spring after drought, giving Tambudzai the hope she had long suppressed. She became a bride celebrated by the village and soon journeyed with her husband to Johannesburg, South Africa, to start a new chapter.

But the promises of a bright future quickly unraveled. What began as bliss turned into betrayal, and what had seemed like safety proved to be yet another trap. A miscarriage, domestic violence, and the brutal revelation of her husband's double life tore apart her heart and shattered her dreams. Her two front teeth were knocked out in a violent rage. Her spirit almost extinguished.

Tambudzai, like many women, learned to mask her pain and bury her trauma deep beneath layers of survival. When she returned to Zimbabwe, she refused to go back to her rural home in Buhera. Harare became her place of escape, where she quietly rebuilt her life through domestic work. She wore resilience like a garment, but inside, she longed to return to her innocence— the girl who once dreamed by the well, who still believed love was safe.

REFLECTION PROMPT

Where have you lost your sense of innocence and trust? What would it take for you to begin the journey of emotional restoration?

AFFIRMATION

I acknowledge the pain of my past, but I choose to heal. I reclaim my innocence and embrace the possibility of love, joy, and wholeness once more.

"He healeth the broken in heart, and bindeth
up their wounds."
—PSALM 147:3

CHAPTER
TWO

———

DARK SECRETS

THE STORY OF TASHANA

The alarm buzzed its shrill cry, pulling Tashana from a night of little rest. She groaned and reached out to silence it, her arm flailing under the pillow as the unwelcome sound persisted. After a few frustrated attempts, she sat up and glared at the pink device that mocked her exhaustion. The weight of sleep still tugged at her eyes, but the demands of a new workday offered no mercy. She had secured a major account only days before, one that came with impossible deadlines and the pressure of proving herself. Her male colleagues had failed where she had succeeded, but now she had less than forty-eight hours to deliver perfection.

Chazelle, her daughter, was with her mother. Tashana had moved her there temporarily to focus on work. She was determined to succeed in this new role. Dating was not a priority. Her heart was guarded—tightly locked behind doors built by trauma and betrayal.

HIDDEN WOUNDS, BURIED DREAMS

Tashana had always dreamed of a life filled with love, security, and success. But reality had rewritten those dreams with harsh ink. Her father's betrayal and mysterious death left deep scars. Her mother, falsely accused of his murder, had barely survived the scrutiny, saved only by the legal brilliance of Mr Blake Senior—a respected lawyer and justice advocate. He represented the Brown family pro bono, cleared her mother's name, and never charged a cent. His kindness became the reason Tashana later applied to Blake & Partners after law school.

There, she met Steven Blake Jr., the son who inherited the firm and his father's name—but not his character. He welcomed her, mentored her, and opened doors. Her intelligence and drive earned her praise, and her mixed-race identity fit the firm's attempt at corporate diversity. Tashana admired him, even trusted him. Until the night of the firm's awards gala, when everything changed.

She accepted a drink. She danced. She trusted. But what happened in that hotel room shattered every piece of trust she had. She awoke with foggy memories and a certainty that she had been violated. Confronting him on Monday, she received no remorse—only cold threats, legal intimidation, and a forced resignation.

When she discovered her pregnancy, she emailed him. His response was brutal. He told her to disappear quietly. He reminded her of his father's generosity and threatened to reopen her mother's case if she spoke out. Tashana decided to keep her baby—and the truth—to herself.

A PHOENIX ARISES

The birth of Chazelle changed everything. As Tashana cradled her daughter's tiny body, a new sense of purpose was born. The bitterness and pain didn't vanish, but they quieted in that sacred moment. Her mother came to help, but they danced around the truth. There was peace in the silence, but not healing.

A new job in Los Angeles helped her rebuild. She excelled. Driven by the need to provide for her daughter and reclaim her life, she climbed quickly. Dating, however, was another battlefield. Unable to trust, she broke hearts before they could break hers.

She filled the silence with achievements and learning, eventually discovering a passion for design and brand strategy. When a top firm offered her a new role in New York, she leapt at the opportunity.

HEALING IN SISTERHOOD

Before the move, Tashana joined a single mothers' support group. It was there that healing found her. In a circle of strong yet broken women—executives, survivors, mothers—she found space to feel. Daniella's story of abuse and redemption cracked something open in her. Then Suzanne's courage in the face of workplace harassment gave her strength.

The turning point came during a prayer. Romans 8:1 was read aloud:

"There is therefore now no condemnation to them which are
in Christ Jesus…"

Tashana broke. Years of buried pain spilled out. Her voice returned only to release anger, shame, and the dark secrets she had carried alone. Her facilitator, Chevon, gently asked if she was ready to forgive. Slowly, through tears, she nodded.

She recommitted her life to faith. Daily spiritual disciplines became her oxygen. She didn't have all the answers, but she had light. And that was enough.

When she moved to New York, she took with her a renewed sense of self, a reawakened spirit, and the quiet fire of hope.

REFLECTION PROMPT

What pain have you carried alone for too long? What would it look like to invite healing into that space?

AFFIRMATION

I am not defined by what hurt me. I rise above the pain, whole and empowered to love again.

"He healeth the broken in heart, and bindeth
up their wounds."
—PSALM 147:3

CHAPTER
THREE

THE ESSENCE OF LOVE

Tambudzai and Tashana's stories may have unfolded continents apart, but the threads that tie them together run deep. Both women were shaped by love—its promises, its betrayals, its absence, and ultimately, its power to heal. Tambudzai longed for love as an escape from hardship, only to encounter pain in its name. Tashana sought to rise above her past, only to be wounded by those she trusted most. Yet, through these dark alleys, both women eventually encountered a different kind of love—one rooted not in fantasy, dependency, or manipulation, but in truth, healing, and spiritual awakening.

It is this deeper understanding of love that this chapter seeks to explore. If we are to truly become whole women, we must understand what love is and what it is not.

"There is a significant difference between a person who desires a covenant relationship with you and one who wants a convenient relationship with you."

—THE CONNECTION FACTOR FOR PERSONAL GROWTH: UNLOCKING YOUR TRUE POTENTIAL THROUGH MEANINGFUL RELATIONSHIPS (CH. 5)

RELATIONSHIP ROLE MODELS

Growing up, I had very few role models who reflected what I now understand to be godly love relationships. The models I admired were distant, and many local examples were steeped in dysfunction. In *Destination Wholeness: Going Beyond Brokenness*, I share personal reflections of childhood experiences that shaped my understanding of love and connection. Escaping into novels became a coping mechanism—but fantasy offered no preparation for real love's complexity.

Thankfully, spiritual communities like Scripture Union and Dunamis Youth Ministries began to ground my worldview in biblical truth.

There, I encountered teachings that offered a healthier lens through which to view relationships and self-worth.

THE FOUR BIBLICAL LOVES

To truly understand love's essence, we must begin with the Creator. The Bible, written in Greek, gives us four foundational types of love:

1. **Eros—Romantic, Sensual Love**

   Rooted in physical attraction, Eros is celebrated within marriage. Outside of covenant, it can lead to confusion and soul ties.

2. **Storge—Familial Love**

   This is the natural affection between parents and children, siblings, and extended family. It teaches loyalty and duty.

3. **Philia—Brotherly Love**

   Deep friendship and emotional intimacy fall under Philia. It's mutual, built on trust, and essential in meaningful relationships.

4. **Agape—Unconditional, Divine Love**

   Agape is God's perfect love—selfless, sacrificial, and eternal. It's the love that Jesus modeled, and the one we're called to reflect.

"By this shall all men know that ye are my disciples, if ye have love one to another."

—JOHN 13:35 (KJV)

Additional Greek Loves: Shades of the Heart

Beyond the biblical framework, Greek thought offers further distinctions that help us assess how we give and receive love:

5. **Ludus—Playful Love**

   Flirtation, light-hearted affection, and courtship. While delightful, it lacks depth without grounding.

6. **Mania—Obsessive Love**

An unhealthy attachment rooted in insecurity. It often leads to co-dependency and emotional instability.

7. **Pragma—Enduring Love**

Mature, committed love built over time. Seen in long-term marriages and seasoned friendships.

8. **Philautia—Self-Love**

Healthy self-regard that enables us to love others well. As Aristotle said,

---

"All friendly feelings for others are an extension of a man's feelings for himself."

Why We Need Love

Love is foundational to human existence. Maslow's hierarchy positions love and belonging just after basic needs. Without it, our development—emotional, relational, and even spiritual—remains stunted.

We seek love to:
- Feel secure and connected
- Be seen and accepted
- Experience purpose through nurturing and being nurtured

Understanding Affection: Love in Action

Affection is love made visible. It's the hug that says "I see you," the phone call that whispers "I care," and the presence that assures "I'm here."

Affection:
- Reinforces emotional bonds
- Varies in intensity depending on the relationship
- Is crucial for emotional health and resilience

SHOWING AFFECTION: PRACTICAL ACTS OF LOVE

- **Verbal:** Words of encouragement, affirmation
- **Physical:** Hugs, holding hands, acts of service
- **Time:** Presence, attention, shared experiences

Whether in romantic or platonic relationships, affection sustains connection. It is the glue of intimacy and the language of love.

REFLECTION PROMPT

- Which type(s) of love have most shaped your story so far? Are there any that you need to heal from or grow in?
- What role does affection play in how you give and receive love today?

AFFIRMATION

I am worthy of a love that is pure, healing, and true. I release false narratives and open my heart to divine, healthy connections that reflect God's best for my life.

CHAPTER
FOUR

SELF-ESTEEM
AND SELF-WORTH

One of the key themes of the first book in this series, *The Connection Factor for Personal Growth: Unlocking Your True Potential Through Meaningful Relationships*, focuses on the importance of connecting with your essential self before attempting to connect with the essential selves of others. This foundational principle is especially relevant for women, many of whom grapple with low self-esteem and diminished self-worth as a result of societal expectations, traumatic experiences, and limiting beliefs.

Negative messages, physical illness, stressful life events, and childhood trauma often shape a woman's internal dialogue. Low self-esteem, in many cases, is both a cause and a consequence of depression. It may manifest as a victim mentality or a deep-rooted inability to assert one's needs, dreams, and dignity.

Our internal world—the mind—is the birthplace of both our battles and our breakthroughs. Romans 12:2 reminds us that spiritual transformation begins with the renewing of the mind. This is where our self-perception takes root. The enemy often launches his fiercest attacks here, where our behaviour begins. Our internal monologue either affirms our divine identity or sabotages it.

How do you see yourself? Through the eyes of others, or through the eyes of God?

KNOWING YOUR SELF-WORTH

Self-worth is more than confidence; it is our internal estimation of our own value. It is shaped in our earliest interactions, long before we can articulate it. In *Destination Wholeness: Going Beyond Brokenness*, I share my own childhood story—marked by neglect, abuse, and pain—and how those early years chipped away at my sense of value.

Research affirms that secure early attachments help children regulate emotions and develop a healthy sense of self-worth. But when parenting is inconsistent, abusive, or emotionally unavailable, that foundation is compromised. Add to that the gendered expectations placed on girls, and the result is an ever-elusive chase for perfection and approval.

Many women are trapped between two extremes: adhering to feminine stereotypes and being labelled weak, or breaking them and being branded unfeminine. The bar keeps shifting, and the cost is a fractured sense of identity. Over time, women internalise shame, develop imposter syndrome, and downplay their achievements to maintain social favour.

We must change the script.

Misery Loves Company

Women with low self-esteem often settle in relationships that confirm their self-doubt. They may avoid healthier connections for fear of exposure or rejection. Adolescents, particularly girls, face additional pressures from media images that reinforce unattainable ideals. The cycle becomes self-perpetuating: low self-worth begets unhealthy choices that reinforce shame and diminish hope.

But this is not a life sentence.

Steps to Reclaim Self-Esteem

Every woman can make intentional choices to build her self-esteem. Here are key steps:

1. **Capture Negative Thoughts**
   Take control of your mental environment. Philippians 4:8 urges us to dwell on things that are noble, pure, and praiseworthy. Change begins by becoming aware of destructive thought patterns.

2. **Know Yourself**
   Understand your preferences, values, and emotional triggers. Learn how past experiences have shaped you.

3. **Care for Yourself**
   Self-esteem grows when we nourish our bodies, minds, and spirits. Prioritise rest, exercise, joy, and spiritual renewal.

4. Respect Yourself

Uphold your values even in the face of external pressure. Practice assertiveness and build trust in your own decisions.

5. Accept Yourself

Embrace your humanity—imperfections, mistakes, and all. Cultivate self-compassion and forgiveness.

6. Love Yourself

Create healthy boundaries. Celebrate your strengths. Treat yourself as you would a beloved friend.

Confident women set healthy boundaries. They don't abandon themselves in relationships. They show up fully, and walk away when a connection demands they shrink to fit.

THE INNER CEILING

The real glass ceiling isn't only in boardrooms—it's in the mind. When women reclaim their identity and rewrite the internal script, they rise. Leadership, boldness, and influence begin with self-worth.

We may not be able to change our past or biology, but we can change our narrative. By reconnecting with our true selves—our values, passions, and purpose—we shift from performing for approval to living from intrinsic worth.

Self-worth is inner security. It's the friend who reminds you of your value in the silence. It's the fire that warms you when external applause fades.

PRAYER AND BLESSING

May God grant you the strength and boldness to set healthy boundaries and connect to your authentic self. In every place of brokenness, may you receive healing and restoration. May your confidence be rooted in Christ, who loves you eternally and unconditionally.

REFLECTION PROMPTS

- What internal narratives about your worth do you need to challenge?
- Which of the six steps above do you feel led to focus on this week?

AFFIRMATION

I am fearfully and wonderfully made. I release shame, comparison, and fear. I embrace my worth, walk in boldness, and honour my true self with love and compassion.

---—---

THE WOMAN AND HER NETWORKS

"I believe that when people connect their aspirations with who they are and what they do, something incredible happens…a seed of greatness begins to flourish, pushing its way through the soil of success. When connected with others, who within their own spheres of influence are experiencing a similar process, something even more extraordinary happens—it changes the way we do life. Our collective contributions increase…communities and industries develop, nations progress and prosper, until humanity as a whole advances."

—DR. CINDY TRIMM

We are living in a world defined by hyperconnectivity—yet paradoxically, many feel more isolated than ever before. Our sensory world has been altered by devices that plug us in and tune us out. Technology has shifted how we relate, often replacing presence with performance, and conversation with curated content. The rise of digital engagement has, in many ways, cost us personal connection.

As Robert J. Putnam revealed in his landmark book *Bowling Alone*, social capital—the networks of relationships among people—is steadily declining. Fewer of us join clubs, attend community meetings, or even know our neighbours. Women, traditionally seen as the glue of communal relationships, now face the triple strain of career, family, and societal expectations, which often leaves little room for nurturing personal networks.

Yet, research consistently shows that social connection is a cornerstone of mental, emotional, and even physical well-being. Strong social networks enhance life quality, boost immunity, promote resilience, and even increase longevity.

WOMEN AND FRIENDSHIP

Landmark studies, such as those conducted by Laura Klein and Shelley Taylor, reveal that women respond to stress through connection. When stressed, women tend to "tend and befriend"—nurturing those around them and seeking out friendships—thanks in part to the release of oxytocin, the bonding hormone.

Another critical study by David Spiegel on women with breast cancer found that those with strong friendship networks lived significantly longer than those without. Harvard's *Nurses' Health Study* confirmed that the more close friends a woman has, the healthier and more content she is likely to be.

In the face of life's storms—loss, transition, or trauma—women with close friends fare better. Friendships become lifelines, safe spaces where stories are shared and healing begins. However, in the busyness of life, many women sideline friendships, prioritizing work and family, often at the expense of their emotional well-being. We must learn to value and invest in these sacred bonds.

The Power of Healthy Friendships:
- Enhance life satisfaction
- Strengthen immunity
- Improve mental health
- Boost longevity
- Foster optimism and resilience
- Support trauma recovery
- Create a sense of belonging and safety

But not all friendships are healthy. Some deplete rather than replenish. A good friend should support your journey, not stall your growth. If a relationship consistently leaves you feeling small, it may be time to press pause—or delete.

NETWORKING VS. FRIENDSHIP: DRAWING THE LINE

In today's professional world, networking is no longer optional—it's essential. But as women, we often blur the line between genuine connection and strategic positioning. Karen Burns, in her book *The Amazing Adventures of Working Girl*, suggests that many women need to develop a clearer boundary between networking and friendship. Networking is not about selling out your authenticity—it's about showing up prepared, confident, and value-aligned.

Helen Fisher, Ph.D., biological anthropologist and author of Why Him, Why Her, explains that men and women network differently. Men tend to be transactional and goal-driven, while women often take a more relational approach. Recognising these differences can help women navigate professional spaces more effectively, without losing their personal essence.

ARE YOU NETWORKING OR SELF-PROMOTING?

Networking has tangible outcomes—career advancement, resource access, collaboration, visibility, and mentorship. Especially for women in male-dominated industries, intentional networking opens doors that talent alone cannot. The difference between networking and self-promotion lies in purpose. Are you building bridges or just broadcasting?

SOCIAL MEDIA AND YOUR DIGITAL FOOTPRINT

Today, our networks extend beyond physical gatherings. Social media has revolutionized the way we connect, learn, and grow. But it has also introduced new challenges. Your digital presence is your personal brand—it speaks long before you say a word.

DIGITAL BRANDING TIPS FOR WOMEN:

1. **Be Positive**—Avoid negativity about past employers, colleagues, or life events.
2. **Stay Consistent**—Ensure your social profiles align with your professional resume.

3. **Be Mindful of Connectivity**—Understand how posts on one platform may sync with others.

4. **Align with Your Aspirations**—Use platforms to reflect your passions, strengths, and purpose.

Social media gives women a chance to shape their narrative. But with this opportunity comes responsibility. Oversharing, inappropriate imagery, profanity, or digital venting can damage your credibility.

GUARDING YOUR DIGITAL IMAGE:

- Avoid racist or profane content
- Don't post during work hours excessively
- Fact-check before posting
- Edit for grammar and tone
- Protect your privacy and others' confidentiality

DISCONNECTING FROM TOXIC NETWORKS

Connection is powerful—but not all connections are healthy. Toxic networks can drain energy, stifle growth, and perpetuate self-doubt. Recognising toxicity is the first step to healing.

Signs of Toxic Relationships:

- Controlling behavior
- Disrespect of boundaries
- One-sided giving
- Constant need to be right
- Chronic dishonesty
- Victim mentality
- Avoidance of responsibility

These patterns, left unchallenged, can infiltrate your mindset and stall your destiny. You cannot always change others—but you can choose whom you allow into your inner circle.

NURTURING LIFE-GIVING CONNECTIONS

In a world that pulls us in a thousand directions, cultivating strong, life-giving networks is a radical act of self-care. Whether digital or face-to-face, intentional relationships help us thrive. As women, we need safe spaces to grow, share, challenge, and heal together.

"Bad company corrupts good morals."
—1 CORINTHIANS 15:33

REFLECTION PROMPT

- Which relationships in your life fuel your purpose—and which drain it?
- Are there connections you need to cultivate, and others you need to release?

AFFIRMATION

I honour the networks that nourish my soul and align with my purpose. I walk in wisdom, connecting with people who reflect God's goodness and vision for my life.

CHAPTER
SIX

THE WOMAN AND HER
ROMANTIC RELATIONSHIPS

As I prepared to write this chapter, I had many thoughts swirling in my mind. I wondered about the kind of women who would read this book—what they might be looking for in life, in love, and in themselves. I also realized that men, too, may find value in these pages. Still, this chapter is specifically dedicated to deep, purpose-driven women—those who long for meaningful romantic connections with men who see and cherish them for who they are, not merely for what they offer.

In my life coaching practice, I've worked with strong women of worth—intelligent, ambitious, visionary, and focused—who often struggle to find men capable of loving them without competing with or projecting insecurity onto them. My heart goes out to those women who have been short-changed in love—who've compromised their standards to accommodate men unwilling to fully value or commit to them. This is not to say that we as women, myself included, are without flaws. Sometimes our own character or emotional patterns can become stumbling blocks. But when a woman knows her worth, she should not have to lower herself to be loved.

KNOWING THE DIFFERENCE BETWEEN BOYS AND MEN

Before a woman settles into a relationship, she must be able to distinguish between a boy who wants to play and a man who is ready to build. Too many women endure heartbreak from males who have aged but not matured. Inspired by my personal experiences and the many stories I've heard, I share this guide adapted from journalist Neha Borkar's article on the key distinctions between boys and men:

1. **A boy fights over petty things. A man knows how to argue constructively.**
2. **Boys fear commitment. Men embrace it.**
3. **Boys are possessive. Men are protective.**
4. **Boys disregard time and money. Men value both.**
5. **Boys dress down. Men dress for the occasion.**
6. **Boys are confused. Men are clear and decisive.**

7. Boys seek 'hotness.' Men seek depth and companionship.
8. Boys play games. Men are direct.
9. Boys fear rejection. Men persevere.
10. Boys blame others. Men take responsibility.
11. Boys avoid deep conversations. Men engage and listen.

DEEP WOMEN AND THEIR NEEDS

Not every man can handle a deep woman. The deeper a woman's soul, the harder it may be for her to find someone who can meet her emotional and intellectual intensity. Rania Naim writes compellingly about why deep women are often misunderstood. Here are five of her key observations:

1. **Deep women crave deep relationships.**
2. **They ask soul-searching questions.**
3. **They are brutally honest.**
4. **They demand consistency.**
5. **They love fully or not at all.**

MISTAKES WOMEN MAKE IN RELATIONSHIPS

Even strong women can make mistakes that sabotage their romantic pursuits. Here are seven common ones:

1. **Not knowing your value.**
2. **Trying to tie him down too soon.**
3. **Over-relying on masculine energy.**
4. **Turning him into a project.**
5. **Failing to appreciate.**
6. **Trust and respect issues.**
7. **Looking for a man to "complete" you.**

THE CHALLENGE OF STRONG WOMEN FINDING LOVE

Strength is beautiful, but it can also be intimidating. Here are ten traits that, while empowering, can make romantic connections more complex:

1. **Strong women don't settle.**
2. **They speak up.**
3. **They don't need a man to complete them.**
4. **They know how to walk away.**
5. **They don't tolerate being options.**
6. **They don't follow traditional dating rules.**
7. **They handle rejection with resilience.**
8. **They ask tough questions.**
9. **They've known heartbreak.**
10. **They don't seek external validation.**

For Dating or for Marriage?

Marriage is a serious commitment. Women should be cautious of the following types of men:

1. **The man without a work ethic.**
2. **The mama's boy.**
3. **The chronic complainer.**
4. **The master manipulator.**
5. **The man with no vision or plan.**

Connections and Guarded Hearts

Many women have been hurt and now guard their hearts. Guarded hearts are not closed—they are cautious. They open slowly, requiring consistent action rather than empty promises. Brendan Burchard said, "Sometimes in our self-protection, we block out the very thing we want so much—connection."

If you are falling for someone with a guarded heart:
- Be patient.
- Be consistent.
- Let love unfold on their terms.

CULTIVATING INTIMACY IN RELATIONSHIPS

Intimacy is not a moment—it's a journey of connection. It is:

- Talking deeply
- Thinking together
- Touching meaningfully
- Being together intentionally

Women often find talking easier than men, but both partners must learn each other's language of intimacy. True intimacy can only flourish where there is trust and healed hearts.

REFLECTION PROMPT

- Which of these relationship insights resonate most with your experience?
- What boundaries or beliefs do you need to revisit to experience healthier love?

AFFIRMATION

I am worthy of love that honors my depth, respects my worth, and nurtures my soul. I release old patterns and embrace relationships rooted in truth, trust, and mutual growth.

—||—

HER BODY
AND HER SEXUALITY

In a world obsessed with appearances, it's remarkable how many of us nurture unhealthy relationships with our own bodies. We compare ourselves to others, often unfairly, and carry self-doubt rooted in distorted ideals of beauty. But our bodies are more than canvases for criticism or competition—they are sacred vessels, intricately crafted by God, designed for wellness, vitality, and purpose.

We may not love every feature, but we can invest in caring for and honouring the uniqueness God gave us. Unfortunately, many women's confidence—and by extension, their ability to connect deeply in relationships—is hindered by their dissatisfaction with their appearance.

THE ROOTS OF BODY DISSATISFACTION

Studies show body dissatisfaction begins alarmingly early. Girls as young as 4 report wishing for thinner bodies. Later in life, this dissatisfaction can follow women into their most intimate spaces. In marriage counselling, it's often revealed that women experience more distracting, anxious thoughts about their bodies during sex—diminishing not only pleasure but confidence, too.

Body image touches every dimension of our lives—emotionally, spiritually, sexually—and its effects are amplified in women struggling with infertility or unresolved trauma. What we believe about our bodies has the power to strengthen or sabotage our relationships.

THE DANGERS OF SELF-OBJECTIFICATION

Across cultures and generations, the female form has been admired, exploited, and too often reduced to objectification. But the danger multiplies when women internalize this lens—seeing themselves not as whole beings, but as a collection of parts to critique or parade.

This is self-objectification: a learned behaviour rooted in societal messages that condition women to value themselves based on appearance. It manifests through constant mirror-checking, photo obsession, social comparison, and body shaming. While it may seem harmless, it has serious consequences—correlated with depression, anxiety, disordered eating, and chronic dissatisfaction.

Even when praise is involved, the pressure of being objectified (by others or self) can pull our attention away from purpose and fulfilment. Objectification theory highlights how these patterns lower self-esteem and inhibit our capacity to be present, vulnerable, and connected in our relationships.

"The treatment of women as sexual objects leads to treating oneself as an object to be evaluated."
—FREDRICKSON & ROBERTS, 1997

BODY IMAGE, SEXUAL SATISFACTION & RELATIONSHIP HEALTH

When self-worth is entangled with body shame, it affects sexual satisfaction and relationship quality. According to Murray's Risk Regulation Model, individuals with a negative self-concept struggle to trust that they're accepted by their partners. This distrust leads to withholding, emotional guardedness, and a decline in intimacy.

In contrast, when a woman has a positive body image and self-concept, she is more confident, open to emotional and physical closeness, and more likely to engage in relationship-enhancing behaviours. Nurturing a healthy relationship with our bodies is not vanity—it's emotional and relational stewardship.

WOMEN AND SEXUAL INTEGRITY

Women are often assumed to be less susceptible to sexual struggles than men—but that's misleading. While men's battles are often visual and physical, women's battles often begin in the heart and mind. Emotional fulfilment is a gateway to sexual vulnerability.

Sexual integrity is not just about physical purity—it's about alignment across all aspects of our being: body, mind, heart, and spirit. When even one of these is out of sync, we experience discontent, compromise, or emotional pain. Guarding our hearts and thoughts (as Proverbs 4:23 advises) is crucial to our wholeness.

"Our sexuality isn't what we do—it's who we are."

In our pursuit of love, many women compromise sexually in hopes of receiving emotional intimacy. But giving sex to get love rarely yields the fruit we long for. Instead, it often births regret, shame, or confusion. Sexuality is a gift meant for covenant, not bargaining.

- Have you ever engaged in sexual activity to feel loved or accepted? What was the outcome?
- Have you felt ashamed of your sexual desires? What beliefs shaped that shame, and are they rooted in truth?
- Where have you set boundaries for sexual integrity, and what anchors those boundaries?

A Word on Wholeness

You are a sexual being by design—not just in body, but in soul and spirit. Sexuality is not shameful; it's sacred. Whether you're married, single, or celibate by choice or circumstance, your body and desires are not flaws to suppress but parts of you to honour and steward wisely.

Prayer:

Almighty God and Father,

I trust You for my every need. Please give me wisdom and courage as I seek fulfilment for my emotional and sexual needs. And above all, keep me connected to You—draw me ever closer—so that I may know where my true fulfilment comes from.

Amen.

WOMEN
AND ABUSIVE RELATIONSHIPS

When many people hear that someone is in an unhealthy or abusive relationship, their first question is, "Why don't they leave?" If you've never been through an abusive relationship, this sort of response might seem logical. Just throw the deuces up and move on with your life—right? But here's the thing—when it comes to relationship abuse, it's never as easy as "just leaving."

Leaving an abusive relationship is hard for many reasons. I have shared here 8 of the many reasons that someone in an unhealthy or toxic situation might stay with their partner:

1. **Society normalizes unhealthy behaviour** so people may not understand that their relationship is abusive. When you think that unhealthy or abusive behaviours are normal, it's hard to identify your relationship as abusive and therefore there's no reason to seek help.

2. **Emotional abuse destroys your self-esteem**, making it feel impossible to start fresh. Oftentimes, people in emotionally abusive relationships may not understand that they are being abused because there's no violence involved. Also, many will dismiss or downplay emotional abuse because they don't think it's as bad as physical abuse. It's hard for those in abusive relationships to leave their partners after they've continuously been made to feel worthless and like there's no better option for themselves.

3. **The Cycle of Abuse:** After every abusive incident comes a make-up honeymoon phase. Often when an abusive situation happens, it is followed by the abuser doing something nice or apologizing and promising that they will never do it again. This makes their partner minimize the original abusive behaviour.

4. **It's dangerous to leave.** Many times, leaving an abusive relationship is not only emotionally difficult, but can also be life-threatening. In fact, the most dangerous time in an abusive relationship is post break-up.

According to the report *Myths & Facts about Domestic Violence* published by the Domestic Violence Intervention Program in 2016, women are 70 times more likely to be killed in the weeks after leaving their abusive partner than at any other time during the relationship.

5. **They feel personally responsible for their partner or their behaviour.** After a conflict, an abuser will turn the situation around and make their partner feel guilty or as though they are somehow at fault. This type of behaviour is known as *gaslighting*.

6. **They believe that if they stick it out, things might change.** A lot of people in abusive relationships stay in them because they love their partner and think that things will change. They might also believe their partner's behaviour is due to tough times or feel as though they can change their partner if they are a better partner themselves.

7. **Fear of how others will react.** People in abusive relationships often feel embarrassed to admit that their partner is abusive for fear of being judged, blamed, marginalized, pitied or looked down on.

8. **They share a life together.** Marriage, children, and shared finances are often huge reasons that people in abusive relationships stay in them. This dependency is heightened in relationships where one partner is differently abled.

There are lots of elements that influence a person's decision to stay in an abusive relationship. And while seeking help to get out of these relationships is the most important thing, blaming someone in an abusive relationship is never okay. There is a big difference between judgment and responsibility. While someone might have used bad judgment by staying in an unhealthy or dangerous situation, it does not mean that they are responsible, or asking, for the abuse perpetrated against them.

RECOGNIZING RED FLAGS: EARLY WARNING SIGNS

Many abusive dynamics start subtly. Here are some early red flags to look out for:

- Extreme jealousy masked as concern
- Monitoring or controlling your phone, whereabouts, or time
- Insisting on quick commitment (e.g. moving in or marriage)
- Isolation from friends and family
- Dismissive comments about your goals, appearance, or emotions
- Love bombing followed by devaluation

If any of these behaviours show up early in a relationship, they are not to be ignored. These seemingly small things often escalate into full-blown control, manipulation, or abuse.

A GLIMPSE INTO HER STORY: THE SILENCE BEHIND THE SMILE

"At first, it was just small things," she said, twirling the strap of her handbag. "He didn't like the friends I kept, so I stopped seeing them. He didn't want me posting online, so I stopped sharing. He wanted to know where I was all the time—it felt like he cared... until it felt like I couldn't breathe without permission."

Stories like hers are not uncommon. Women stay silent, wear a brave smile, and slowly disappear behind the shadows of someone else's control. It's not because they are weak, but because their strength has been slowly dismantled.

FINDING A WAY OUT: STEPS TOWARD HEALING AND SAFETY

For those feeling trapped or unsure, here are a few first steps:

- **Create a safety plan**: Identify safe people and places; keep emergency documents and essentials in an accessible, hidden location.
- **Talk to someone you trust**: A therapist, pastor, counselor, or support group can help you process and plan.
- **Document the abuse**: If it's safe to do so, keep records of texts, emails, or photos that can be helpful later.

- **Connect with local resources**: Women's shelters, domestic violence hotlines, and legal advocates are there to help.

Leaving is not the end—it's the beginning of reclaiming your identity, safety, and wholeness.

FINAL THOUGHTS AND A PRAYER

Having a personal understanding of what it means to be in an abusive relationship, my prayer is that God would grant you wisdom, boldness, courage and strength to know when the season for a relationship has ended. Living a life of perpetual fear and bondage is definitely not God's best for you. May you surround yourself with sound counsel that will guide you to a place of safety and wholeness as you pursue fulfilling relationships.

Prayer:

Father God,

Please give me the discernment to see things clearly, the strength to walk in truth, and the courage to seek freedom where I have felt confined. Heal every place of brokenness within me and grant me the grace to pursue a life of peace, dignity, and love. Amen.

THE WOMAN, HER FAITH AND HER LEGACY

INTIMACY WITH GOD

Intimacy with God might sound like a strange concept. How do you become close to someone you can't see, hear, or touch? You can't meet God for coffee or wrap Him in a warm embrace. And yet, the very essence of our creation is rooted in this—God designed us for deep fellowship with Him. But what does that really look like?

Like many believers, I long to know God, hear His voice, and feel His presence guiding my life. Since my spiritual rebirth, I've been on a journey of learning how to pursue intimacy with the God of the universe. God is not a distant deity; He is a living, personal, and mysterious being who desires connection.

> "You will seek me and find me when you seek me
> with all your heart."
> —JEREMIAH 29:13

KEYS TO CONNECTING WITH GOD

1. Desire Intimacy with God

True intimacy begins with desire. Not a casual intention, but a deep, persistent hunger. Is God one item on a long list of goals? Or is He *the* pursuit? David expressed it best:

> "One thing I ask of the Lord... that I may dwell in the house
> of the Lord all the days of my life..."
> —PSALM 27:4

Paul echoed this in Philippians 3:8, counting everything as loss compared to the privilege of knowing Christ intimately.

2. Acknowledge the Supremacy of God

> "The earth is the Lord's, and everything in it..."
> —PSALM 24:1

Acknowledging God as the Source of all allows us to surrender fully. We are created in His image and called to reflect His likeness. We are not just His creation—we are His children. "

> You are little gods and all of you are children of
> the Most High God."
> —PSALM 82:6

3. Accept the Grace of Restoration

Though sin fractured our connection with God, grace restored it. Through the sacrifice of Jesus Christ, we are welcomed back into right relationship. Reconciliation is not earned—it is a gift to be received.

4. Aim for a Personal Relationship

Church attendance and ministry activity are valuable, but they can never replace a personal walk with God. True intimacy requires daily disciplines—prayer, worship, and studying the Word. We must quiet ourselves long enough to *hear* God speak. He longs for conversation with His daughters.

5. Aspire to Find Your Purpose in God

You were not designed to self-generate purpose. Identity and calling are found in your Creator. Ask yourself:

- Do I know my life's purpose?
- Am I walking in my assignment?

- What spheres of influence am I called to impact?

   Purpose is birthed in presence. Your calling will become clearer the more time you spend with the One who formed you.

WHAT DOES YOUR LEGACY LOOK LIKE?

Legacy is more than what you leave behind—it's what you build every day. It's not limited to possessions like houses, land, or wealth. It is reflected in the stories told about you, the lives you've touched, and the values you've instilled.

We all leave a legacy—*intentionally or not*. Legacy is not just inheritance—it is also tradition, habit, and how you made others feel. It's found in both the material and the spiritual, in the eternal imprint we leave on hearts and minds.

We've all seen families torn apart over possessions after a loved one passes. But what of families who inherit wisdom, prayer, joy, and strength of character? A well-lived life is a richer legacy than any bank account.

THE ULTIMATE LEGACY: A LIFE OF FAITH

Jesus left a legacy not of gold or silver, but of *love, sacrifice, and redemption*. He walked the road of Calvary for us. He gave His life so we could live abundantly and eternally. Our highest legacy, then, is to reflect His light in our generation and pass it on.

"Well done, good and faithful servant… enter into the
joy of your Lord."
—MATTHEW 25:23

CRAFTING YOUR LIFE PURPOSE STATEMENTS

To build a lasting legacy, take time to develop life purpose statements in these four key areas:

- **Personal Life**: Your core values, character, wellness, rest, hobbies, and identity.
- **Spiritual Life**: Your faith, service, stewardship, worship, and walk with God.
- **Vocational Life**: Your work, calling, talents, and contributions to society.
- **Relational Life**: Your roles in family, friendships, parenting, marriage, and community.

Let each statement be a step of faith—an anchor for your decisions, dreams, and direction.

FINAL REFLECTION

Your legacy is being written right now, in every choice and every connection. May it be a legacy of **love**, **purpose**, and **faith**.

"Your legacy is every life you've touched. Fill every moment with love, because every moment you are building your legacy."

Prayer:

Heavenly Father,

I surrender every part of my life to You—my past, present, and future. Help me to walk in intimacy with You daily. Let my life bear fruit that glorifies Your name. Grant me grace to leave a legacy of faith, love, and eternal impact. In Jesus' name, Amen.

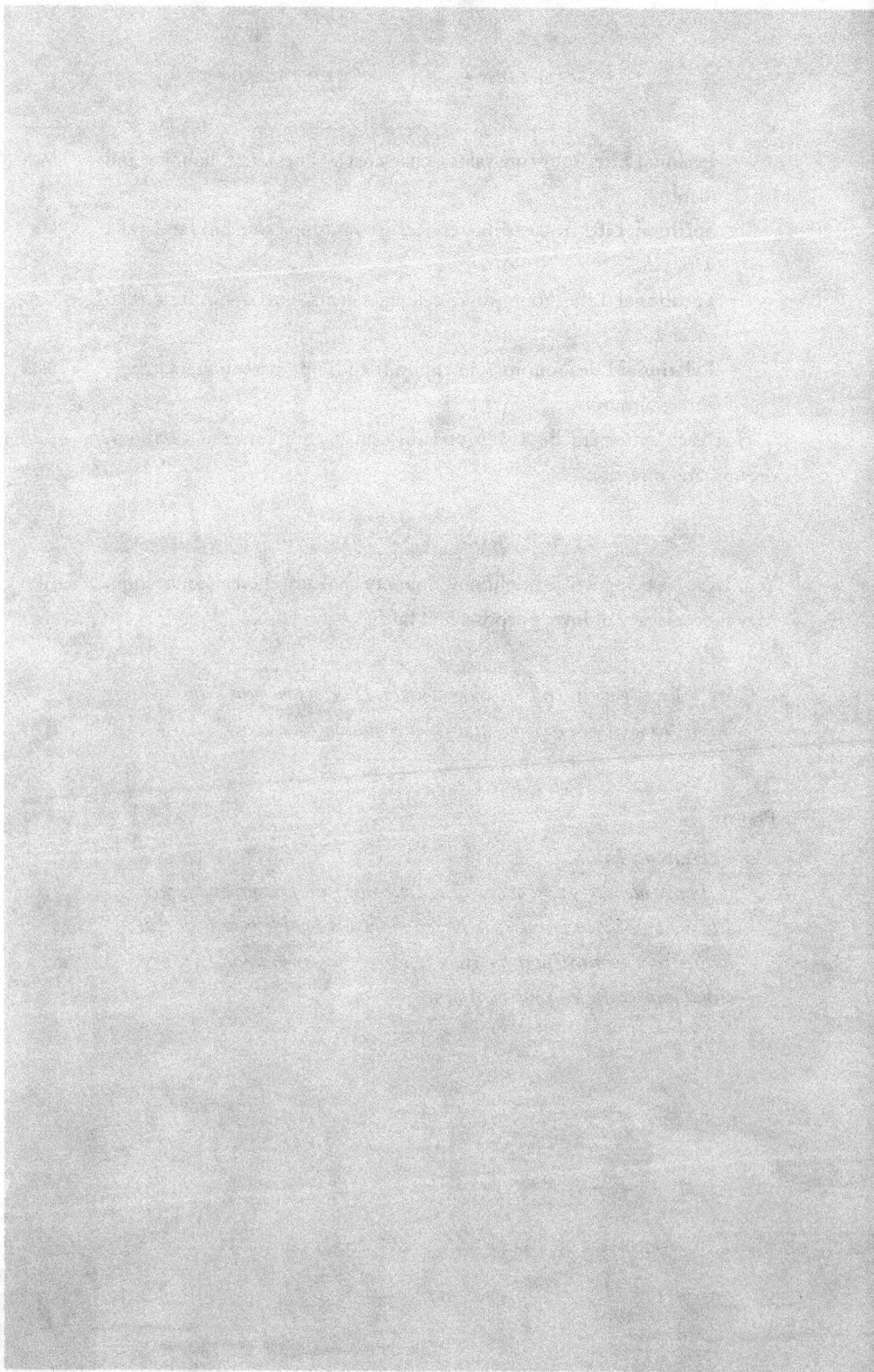

A PRAYER FOR WOMANHOOD, WHOLENESS, AND DIVINE SISTERHOOD

Faithful Father,

Thank You for the gift of womanhood—beautiful, complex, and full of purpose. Thank You for reminding me that connection is not weakness but a sacred strength that nurtures healing, vision, and destiny.

I release every hurt, every comparison, every disappointment I have carried from past relationships. Restore me, O God. Renew my heart, my confidence, and my capacity to love, serve, and trust again.

Surround me with women who speak life, who challenge me to rise, and who walk with me as I become all that You created me to be. Heal the divides. Restore the sisterhood. Teach me to be both supported and supportive.

May I stand as a whole woman—rooted in identity, strengthened by wise connections, and committed to rising and lifting others. Let my life be a testament to what happens when women connect in truth and purpose.

In Jesus' Name,

Amen.

THE CONNECTION FACTOR SERIES

This powerful series by Cynthia Chirinda explores the transformative power of authentic connection—starting from self-awareness and extending to strategic alliances. Titles in the series include:

1. **The Connection Factor for Personal Growth**
   Unlocking Your True Potential Through Meaningful Relationships
   A guide to connecting with yourself and others across personal, professional, and spiritual spheres. Offers practical wisdom for auditing, nurturing, or recalibrating relationships for holistic growth.

2. **The Connection Factor for Women**
   Unlock the Power of Purposeful Connections
   A strategic guide for women to build authentic engagement, overcome relational barriers, and cultivate networks that accelerate growth and legacy-building.

3. **The Connection Factor for Leaders**
   Unlocking Value from Your Strategic Partners
   A relational leadership handbook for qualifying, auditing, and aligning stakeholder relationships for long-term impact and organizational purpose.

Each book in the series is designed to stand alone while weaving together one core truth:

We were never meant to walk alone.

Your growth, purpose, and legacy are nurtured through intentional, life-giving connections.

ABOUT THE AUTHOR

Cynthia Chirinda is a Transformation Catalyst, Systems Change Practitioner, and Personal Development Coach committed to helping individuals and institutions thrive in purpose-driven alignment. Her work bridges faith, leadership, and human development across diverse sectors—from grassroots communities to policy tables.

Through her writing, speaking, and coaching work, Cynthia continues to champion authentic connection as the foundation for wholeness, influence, and impact.

She is the author of several life-shaping books, including:
- *The Connection Factor Series* (Personal Growth, Women, Leaders)
- *Can the Whole Woman Please Stand Up!*
- *Managing Transitions: Navigating Change with Grace*
- *The Whole You—Vital Keys for Balanced Living*
- *Destination Wholeness—Going Beyond Brokenness*
- *You Are Not Damaged Goods* series (*Reboot and Start Afresh, Blossom and Flourish, Transitioning from Tragedies to Triumph*)
- *Clothed By Love*
- *The Wealthy Diary of African Wisdom*
- *Intelligent Conversations—A Mindset Shift Towards a Developed Africa*
- *Whole Enough to Go: Embracing God's Call in Imperfection*

Co-authored works: *Success Within Reach, Reinvented and Victorious: The Anthology*

She is also the visionary behind:
- **Intelligent Conversations with Cynthia**—a transformative broadcast platform for leadership and healing dialogues

- **Women Rising in Africa**—a multimedia series spotlighting women leaders across the continent
- **The Extra Mile**—a documentary tribute to women building nations through courage and faith

Wholeness is not about perfection—it is about courageously embracing each season, becoming rooted in faith, and rising into God-ordained purpose.

Connect with Cynthia:
Website: www.cynthiachirinda.com
Email: info@cynthiachirinda.com
LinkedIn: Cynthia Chirinda